A Poetry Book

HEAD IN THE CLOUDS

MILA ROE

Copyright © 2020 by Milaurys Morales
formally known as Mila Roe

All rights reserved.

Published in the United States of America

ISBN-13: 978-0-578-66322-7

Cover Art by: Steve-V
Instagram: @Stevethomas.design

Author photo: Maurice Manigault

To all the people that can't quite seem to find themselves, you are not alone. These are my heartbreaks, my lessons, my happy times and blessings.

CONTENTS

ADOLESCENCE

Bad Bitch Generation 13
Flaws 16
Monster In My Dreams 18
I'm A Mess 21
Ilsa del Incanto 22
New Age 24
Shine, Baby 26
Fuck Friends 27
Teen Mom 28
A Letter to My Unborn Child 30
Today is A New Day 34
I Promised Myself 35

LOVE/ PAIN

Love 39
Generations 40
Free 42
Crimes 43
Soul Tribe 45
It's Different With You 47

Men 48
All or Nothing 49
It Was Time 50
I Was Dying Inside 51
Wasted Love 52
Feeling Some Type of Way 53
Here I Am 54
I Found Myself 55
The Universe Replied 56
I Should Have Known My Worth 59
Deuces 60
I Still Survived 61
Once Upon A Time 62

BREAKTHROUGH

Feels 67
963 Hz 68
Mal De Ojo 69
Not Yours To Claim 70
Home Sick 72
Care Free 73
Anti-Social 74
Learn 75
The Moon 76

You've Come This Far 77
Only Way Out is Through 78
Hope 79
Missing 82
Today's Affirmation 83
Good For You 84

LESSONS

Dreams Of Wings 89
Jaded 92
Twilight Zone 93
Lights Off 94
Give It Another Try 96
Lessons Life Teach 98
At All Cost 100
Power 101
On My Worst Days 103
Elevate 104
Leap of Faith 105
In This Life 106
Family Ties 108

ADOLESCENCE

Head In The Clouds

in a world full of bad bitches,
i will always choose to be the outcast.

or a Lauryn Hill
looking to be right within.

fuck society's definition of
what makes a woman worthy.

let's take it back to the 90's,
frizzy hair,
mix-match outfits
and natural bodies.

i don't want to be
or act like barbie.

you want to be plastic,
i want to be real.

as down to earth as it gets
with no regrets.

you look at me and think,
"basic."
i look at you and think,
"helpless."

your ancestors
would be ashamed.

stop teaching men to
love your image
more
than your mind.

see,
your image can change,
but your intelligence
will never fade.

the knowledge
you acquire
can take you further
than your body.

Head In The Clouds

i don't want to
be a sex symbol.

just want to be
respected and accepted
for who i am within.

don't be a bad bitch
in designer heels.

be a **smart woman**
with an un-touchable
aura and investments.

teach your daughters
while young
so they'll grow up to
be queens.

let's make this the last
bad bitch generation.

let's plant this new seed.

<u>Bad Bitch Generation.</u>

Mila Roe

chipped toe nails,
thin fragile finger nails.

dead ends,
armpits growing hair.

yellow teeth,
too much coffee.

acne prone face,
not enough water.

Introverted,
yet too friendly.

Head In The Clouds

if only i could find a way to speak.

i was so scared that i peed.

there was a monster in my dreams.

hopeless, alone and confused
lied the nine-year-old me.

with no one who would believe.

took so many awkward stares.

so many nights afraid
looking at the door
and often catching
the monster
just sitting there
watching me.

waiting
for the perfect
time.

took that same monster
to get caught watching
someone else that wasn't me.

for them to realize.

the monster
didn't reside
in my dreams.

now
they believed.

<u>Monster in My Dreams.</u>

Head In The Clouds

i can never keep my shoes clean,
no matter how hard i try.

no matter how valuable i may see them,
i still can't and don't know why.

careful.

there are puddles everywhere.

i look down to watch my steps.

but i always get them wet.

<u>I'm A Mess.</u>

Puerto Rico
oh, how beautiful.

nothing like the first breeze,
the palm trees,
the beach.

what a paradise.

waking up to roosters,
the smell of bustello coffee,
fresh eggs on the skillet.

the way it sings to your taste buds
the way it warms your soul.

the music.

growing up listening
to Marc Anthony
or Celia Cruz.

Head In The Clouds

playing in streams.

riding horses on the beach.

how about hopping roofs
or picking quenepas off the trees.

racing outside barefoot
and living care free.

so many memories.

so overwhelming.

they always
get the best of me.

<u>Isla Del Incanto.</u>

Mila Roe

so much hatred.

so much greed.

such a need
to be the queen.

don't you know
we're all queens.

at the top
we should all be.

holding hands
not fighting over any man.

not calling each other names,
or fighting over individual gains.

if united, we could conquer the world.

Head In The Clouds

teach young girls
what not to fight over.

like money or pearls.

let go of old ways
embrace this new change.

we're all the same beings
we're one and the same.

<u>New Age.</u>

don't be afraid
or ashamed,

to be different.

let your light
shine through.

to reveal
the real you.

<u>Shine, Baby.</u>

Head In The Clouds

i have tried the whole friend thing
and it never works out.

i guess i am just too real
or **too raw.**

i always end up
with no friends.

after running my mouth.

i don't like the fake stuff.

if i feel something is off
i will **tell you about** it.

i'm not afraid to hide it,
not afraid of confrontation.

although i'd rather
live without it.

<u>Fuck Friends.</u>

Mila Roe

young and careless.

living with no worries, no bills.

exposed to parties, alcohol, drugs and sexting.

text's like

"my moms at work, come over
 let's have a session."

turned into blunts sparked, loud music and heavy sexting.

no condoms.
it's just us, so who needs protection?

month's pass with no moon cycle.
followed by a doctor's visit and stressing.

here comes the positive pregnancy test
that's supposed to be a blessing.

Head In The Clouds

now here i am **stressing.**

first thought is, "my mom is going to kill me"
next one is, "am i ready for this?"

what about college and living in a dorm room?

now, with my baby i will share a room.

young and careless.

i used to be fearless.

now i want to curl up into a ball and hide.

such a shame, babies having babies.

life will never be the same.

Teen Mom.

it wasn't time, said it wasn't time.

it wasn't mine yet, so it was justified.

this thing that grew inside, an invasion

on my body, on my heart, on my mind.

i felt it growing, with each day that passed.

so unexpected, so unplanned.

such a crime, i committed.

it wanted to stay alive.

Head In The Clouds

SO SELFISH
SO SELFISH
SO SELFISH.

I HATE THIS
I HATE THIS
I HATE THIS.

i wish i could have kept it.

a life so unplanned, so unknown.

who knows what could of been.
i guess now, we'll never know.

only he knows my pain.

the tears i cried, the vicious screams
i held inside.

the memory of cold tools entering me.
the way i felt when i felt it leave.

i will burn in hell for all eternity.

there's no saving me.

Head In The Clouds

i guess i will never get to meet you.

i hope the angels greeted you.
cradled you and treated you
like a mother should.

like i was supposed to.

so selfish, so stuck in my ways.

i will take this pain with me
to the grave.

<u>A Letter to My Unborn Child.</u>

i am not my mistakes.

i am not yesterday.

i will let all my sins drift away.

Today is A New Day.

Head In The Clouds

i promised myself, i will smile
through the ups and downs.

i promised myself, i will always
stand tall and ready for another round.

i promised myself i will fight.

no matter how many times
my knees hit the ground.

i promised myself i will be here
for myself when no-one else is around.

I Promised Myself.

LOVE / PAIN

Head In The Clouds

it was the first time,
i felt a sharp pain in my gut.

tears pouring,
causing thunderstorms in my eyes.

flower petals slowly falling.

soul dying
heart pounding.

that is when i truly felt
love.

<u>Love.</u>

Mila Roe

she was never taught to love herself-
at least not fully.

was reminded daily of her outer beauty,
just never the beauty she held **within.**

she never learned what real love
was supposed to be.

or what it looked like.

all she's seen were bruises
bad fights and infidelity.

was told to have self-love
by a woman who often
forgot to have any.

Head In The Clouds

fatherless
misguided and misunderstood.

her grandmother, mother and herself.

three generations later and a repeated cycle.

will she be the one to break this curse?

will her children continue it?

when does it end?

how does she

begin?

<u>Generations.</u>

Mila Roe

you make me feel free.

there's no other place
i'd rather be,

but here,

under the stars with you
staring at the moon.

thinking about
all the great things

we could do.

<u>Free.</u>

Head In The Clouds

last night, i tasted his soul.

bitter and heartless

who made him so cold?

well,

never mind the question.

let's get straight to this intervention.

ring finger on his third eye

right hand on his chest.

healing energy

transferred into him.

made love to his mind.

got rid of the pain.

i erased all the crimes

she committed.

now his soul is mine.

<u>Crimes.</u>

Head in The Clouds

a love like this,
takes **lifetimes**
to build.

but we managed
to do it
in half of a decade.

i look into your eyes
and i am more than certain,

there's no breaking ties.
there's no more lies.

no more egos
or entitlements.

putting all
our pride
to the side.

nothing left,
but **peace of mind.**

deep love and understanding
is what we feel inside.

went and made it
through the struggles.

now it's time
to let our love
shine.

you've become
my soul family.

so i'm always
down to ride.

<u>Soul Tribe.</u>

Head In The Clouds

i love how comfortable

i am with you.

lying in bed, naked.

uncovered.

unbothered.

you looking at me

as if i were a flower.

growing **beautifully**

through concrete.

It's Different With You.

"all men look."
he says.

but all i heard was
"men aren't shit."

how could he say that to me?

he makes me want to scream.

pack up all my shit and leave.

this isn't even me.

and it damn sure isn't

how love's supposed to be.

<u>Men.</u>

Head In The Clouds

it looks like you want to mean it.

like you battle your thoughts
and make yourself believe it.

do you really want this,
or do you just feel stuck?

because lately,
your kisses have been cold,
like running away is a must.

if you don't want this,
don't waste my time.

say your goodbye's.

go live your life.

<u>All Or Nothing.</u>

i felt my heart crack,
but it wasn't the first time.

you see i have many cracks,
some deeper than others.

but this one, i felt in my soul.

because finally, i realized
it was one crack too many.

no one was coming to save me.

it was time to get my heart back.

it was time, i saved myself.

<u>It Was Time.</u>

Head In The Clouds

it rained so hard,

so hard that it took my need to cry.

the rain drops trickled down the window
as the tears would from my eyes.

<u>I Was Dying Inside.</u>

i mourn you
every day.

but the worst part is,
you're not even dead.

we're just not close
anymore
or friends.

will this feeling ever fade?

if not, i just pray
you feel the same.

<u>Wasted Love.</u>

Head In The Clouds

as the years go by,
i begin to wonder,

will i ever
feel that high
again?

not the high
you feel
from drugs.

no drug
could ever
make me feel
that way.

Feeling Some Type of Way.

Mila Roe

i loved you so much
that it **crippled me.**

now, here i am

ashamed.

afraid to love
or give myself

fully

to anyone else
again.

<u>**Here I Am.**</u>

Head In The Clouds

i lost you.

but, in the process
i found myself.

learned to love myself
and hold myself at night.

i no longer need anyone
to hold me tight.

or tell me everything
is going to be alright.

<u>I Found Myself.</u>

i refused to let him go-
he was mine.

i devoted years
of my life.

pouring greatness
into this man.

so he was mine.

"**i refuse to let him go.**"
i said.

the universe
replied.

but not with words.

i tried, i cried
then cried and tried.

Head In The Clouds

i pleaded,
forgave,
i crashed.

i almost died.

this man i loved,
played games

with my heart
and mind.

from the start i knew
he was no good

i saw it
in his eyes.

the tears
over the years
showered me

then i grew
out of love.

when the tears stopped,
the sun came out.

then i **blossomed.**

now i've healed
i've **grown.**

i've evolved
and it shows.

<u>The Universe Replied.</u>

Head In The Clouds

i gave you my all,

but you played me.

so, there's love lost.

don't come back around
when you realize

they ain't me.

by then,
i'll be long gone.

laughing

because you passed up
a girl that's so wavy.

I Should Have Known My Worth.

it is not your fault.

some men only appreciate
what they do not have.

he is one of those men.

so instead of crying,

make him appreciate you.

sincerely,

the girl he lost
and now appreciates.

<u>Deuces.</u>

Head In The Clouds

i hope one day
you learn to let me go.

but the memory of me
stays with you.

all those times
i put your needs
before mine-

i hope
it eats you up
inside.

to know
that no matter
how many times
you tried
to convince me
i couldn't live
without you.

i still survived.

in the end
we didn't last.

but the memories
are a blast.

i replay them
in my head sometimes.

not because i miss you
or want you back.

but as a reminder
that although, not all love lasts,

i should never grow to hate you
or wish you bad.

because once upon a time,
we were all each other had.

Once Upon A Time.

BREAKTHROUGH

Head In The Clouds

today, i feel alive.

the vibes are just right.
the breeze feels real nice.
the stars shine so bright.

i finally feel like
we're going to be

alright.

<u>Feels.</u>

my intuition bothers people,
i can tell.

but instead of taking it personal,
they should focus.

focus on being more in tune
with themselves.

"it's hard work."

yea, i know.
you just have to take it slow.

just stay focused.
lay back,
relax.

let the 963 hz music
take control.

<u>963 Hz.</u>

Head In The Clouds

careful.

most of them

don't want you
to uncover

your true potential.

<u>Mal De Ojo.</u>

love yourself.

the same way
you want them to.

actually,
no.

love yourself more
than that.

dig deep
into your soul.

while you're there,
hug yourself.

forgive yourself.

Head In The Clouds

for searching
in all the wrong places.

you belong to you.

it's always been that way.

it always will be.

Not Yours to Claim.

life is so precious
and short.

it's here
and then it's not.

we could all be gone
in a matter of seconds.

leaving the ones we love
behind.

i know they would miss me
so i always make it back.

i pray to god that
nothing

keeps me
from coming back.

<u>Home Sick.</u>

Head In The Clouds

the real me.

something not many
get to see.

your presence
did something.

it sparked a fire in me.

instantly,
i let you in.

guess we're both
carefree.

i knew i could trust
you.

i just knew
we were
meant to be.

<u>Care Free.</u>

i don't like social media.

to me,

it's just a big circus.

full of clowns.

bad bitches.

and people with
shallow surfaces.

Anti-Social.

Head In The Clouds

most people will only

let you down.

learn to be

okay with that.

learn to

have your own back.

<u>Learn.</u>

when I'm feeling lost,

i look at the moon.

her light guides me through.

we talk for hours until

i'm no longer feeling blue.

<u>The Moon.</u>

Head In The Clouds

rise up.

from the

ashes.

like the

phoenix

you are.

<u>You've Come This Far.</u>

when the sky seems to be
falling down on you,

and is no longer
bright and blue:

i pray you find
the strength
to make it through.

no need to go
feeling alone.

we're all fighting
our own storms.

just lean on me,
i'll lean on you.

together
we can stop
the rain.

and make the sky
return to baby blue.

<u>Only Way Out is Through.</u>

Head In The Clouds

yesterday,
i was a mess.

but today,
the sun still set.

the birds still dance
in the morning sky.
as if they're glad
the night is gone.

so why can't i
wake up and dance,
in the morning sky

as they have done?

as if the dark night
of my heart is gone.

if the birds can
go around all day
and not get tired,

or find a safe haven
in the night
and wait for hours,
to see the sun
rise up again:

then so can i.

i convinced myself
to rise up.

rise up
like the sun
and shine
my light.

i decided
nobody
and
nothing,

can get
in my way.

Head In The Clouds

i know the dark night
of my heart
will one day soon
have its time again.

and that's okay.

because i know
the sun will always
rise and set
each morning.

giving me hope.

knowing
i'll always
see a new day.

<u>Hope.</u>

sometimes you have to
disappear for a while.

gather yourself
and let them think
what they want.

let them think
your time is over.

when surely
it has yet begun.

<u>Missing.</u>

Head In The Clouds

Today's Affirmation:

i am enough every day.

i am beautiful in every way.

i deserve all of the abundance.

and love.

that continues to come my way.

finally.

you stopped sleeping on yourself.

good for you, for letting go of those
who no longer serve the new you.

for we are all allowed to change
if it means bettering ourselves.

good for you, for allowing
yourself to go wherever
the wind takes you.

for not feeling guilt.

good for you.

for realizing
this life is yours
to live.

<u>Good for You.</u>

LESSONS

Head In The Clouds

i thought i'd never grow.

confined to the ground,

my body so heavy,

i could barely get around.

the floor is always so cold.

high winds, all ice, no snow

there's no way i will ever grow.

my heart is always so warm,

so warm it gives me hope.

i dream of pink skies

white sand, warm toes.

Mila Roe

the sun never shines here.

there's no birds in the sky here.

the trees all die here.

i'm the only thing alive here.

there's no way i'll survive here.

last night, i dreamt of wings

like the ones the caterpillars grew
and used to fly away.

i wanted them so bad

i thought my heart would shatter

making my cause of death heart break.

i need to get away.

Head In The Clouds

i sleep and sleep,

in hopes to dream of wings.

wings to fly away

to a better place

a better time.

a better state of mind.

who am i?

why am i here?

how will i survive?

<u>Dreams Of Wings.</u>

i'm a mother first,
then a wife.

after that
i'm the soul inside of me.

i wake up every morning
and think about feeding everyone
besides me.

i used to dream
of living freely.

backpacking through mountains,
looking to find bits of myself
in everything around me.

but now, i'm just tired
and wired,

from the four cups of coffee
needed to feel inspired.

<u>Jaded.</u>

Head In The Clouds

do you ever feel like,

you've been doing life all wrong?

like there's a noose with your name on it

but you're trying hard to remain strong?

i really am

i promise.

i just feel like i can't continue holding on.

living life in a twilight zone and everyday

something goes wrong.

<u>Twilight Zone.</u>

adults have boogie men too.

they don't care if you have
kids running around.

don't care if you have
food in your house.

that green paper is all
they're worried about.

oh, and when you pay,

you better have the
exact dollar amount.

or they'll come to
your house.

Head In The Clouds

and when they do
there's no working it out.

no help given out.

once them lights go off.

it's up to you to figure it out.

<u>Lights Off.</u>

Mila Roe

please
don't give up.

No matter how hard
life gets.

please don't.

i don't want the tears
to pour from my eyes.
every time i hear your name.

we're all dying a little inside.

talk to me
don't hide.

**don't question
why you're alive.**

Head In The Clouds

don't tell me life's too much.
or that you're too weak to try.

just rest.

lay back.

let's talk a little
to figure out what's inside.

<u>Give It Another Try.</u>

Mila Roe

if you let it,
life can teach you a lot.

i'm not talking just the good
but also the bad.

good experiences make you happy
of course.

but the bad ones teach you:
failure should make you proud.

proud of trying.

and although not succeeding
still believing.

the lessons life teach,

can make your head spin
round and round.

make you want to
scream out loud.

but if you truly
pay attention,

you'll notice that life
does it for a reason.

a bad day is just
a bad day.

but there's many
more days and seasons.

<u>Lessons Life Teach.</u>

nobody
needs you.

more
than you
need you.

so
protect
your energy.

<u>At All Cost.</u>

Head In The Clouds

on my worst days
i just want to feel.

don't tell me
positive things.

let me bathe
in my emotions.

let me cry it all out.
so eventually,

i can heal.

<u>On My Worst Days.</u>

there's a blessing
in every lesson.

just open up your mind

to the possibilities
of learning

through the depression
and hard times.

in order to elevate.
one must first

be patient
and realize:

**good things
take time.**

Elevate.

Head In The Clouds

finally.
i learned to let go.

of everything
that was weighing on me.

took a leap of faith.

then learned to fly.

<u>Leap Of Faith.</u>

in this life, we are living,
it is so easy to get lost.

so easy
to forget who you are,

what you stand for or
where you come from.

we go all day
feeling lost.

but not because
we truly are.

bills piling up
by the day.

leaving no time
to waste.

Head In The Clouds

So, we get up
every morning.
in a haste.

hoping tomorrow
will be a better day.

praying.
that god will help us
find our way and
take us home
one day.

<u>In This Life.</u>

Mila Roe

some of the purest souls i know
are born into complicated families.

myself included, of course.

i taught myself to believe this was
arranged in the heavens, way before earth.

with the intention to teach us things
and create our stories.

some of the purest souls i know,
have the saddest stories to tell.

the ones you learn the biggest
life lessons from and apply
to your own journey.

most of them usually
start with family.

Head In The Clouds

from feuds to verbal, sexual and physical abuse.

to absent moms and dads leaving us mourning
and searching for a love we've never known.

i have known people struggling with
substance abuse and their excuse?

usually starts with family.

in my teen's i was a wanderer.

a girl untamed, lost and left searching
for a long lost father figure in every boy
i believed to be not good enough for me.

out with fake friends
wandering the streets.
but, at least i felt free.

i never went without at home
always had food and clothes.

money was never a problem, i mean
unless my mom was superwoman
and never let it show.

she did amazing raising us.

a broken mom, leaving a known world
and her children's father behind.

so much respect for that courage she had.

we never went without at home, i mean
unless you count the many days and nights
where my heart was broken and even though
my mom was around, i had no-one to talk to.

no-one to run to and get loving hugs from.

being vulnerable with us is just something
she never learned to do.

i blame it on her absent father who clearly
never knew the kind of damage he would do.

like me, she was left wandering too.

the families we are born into
are here to teach us lessons.

lessons that may hurt like hell
and change our perspective.

but important ones.

the kind of lessons
we must pass on through stories.

for those stories help the world.

they help people feel less alone
and shows them that they no longer
have to battle life on their own.

through those stories, they learn to break
boundaries and generational curses.

in this life, i have learned that

the biggest life lessons are learned
through the families we are born into.

and through the voices of those who
always felt unheard.

<u>Family Ties.</u>

IN HONOR OF MY LOVING ABUELITA

mi abuelita,
the sunshine of my day,

the stars in my night sky,
there's nothing like her warm embrace.

nothing like her avena, early morning
before a long day.

the woman who sewed my uniforms
and made my bloody nose runs go away

by simply placing a penny on my forehead
then telling me to sit and stay.

picking herbs out of her garden
and prepping food for the day

i was her babygirl
and no-one could ever get in the way.

i will cherish our memories, forever and a day

<u>Mi Abuelita.</u>

Milaurys Morales- Roe, formally known as Mila Roe, was inspired to write this book while attending a creative writing class at Hudson Valley Community College. Her passion has always been in the arts; She has been a featured artist at several art shows and Art on Lark in Albany, NY. Her love for art and poetry began as a young child; Inspired by the Puerto Rican culture, along with her poetic grandmother. Growing up she always felt like an alien compared to those around her, causing her to feel alone which began the suppression of her thoughts and feelings. Thankfully, she turned that into poetry for the soul. Her mission is to remind readers that they are not alone. We all have skeletons in our closets, dark thoughts, heart-breaks and bad days.

Thank you for going on this journey with me and allowing me to speak freely. I hope you learned something from this.

If you enjoyed this book, please feel free to leave it an honest review. Any review is appreciated, as it helps new readers decide on investing time into it or not.

Much love,

Mila Roe

www.ingramcontent.com/pod-product-compliance
Lightning Source LLC
Chambersburg PA
CBHW031405040426
42444CB00005B/419